THE ART OF CONSCIOUS CONTENTMENT

*A Handbook for Meditation
and Spiritual Freedom*

JEFF CARREIRA

The Art of

CONSCIOUS CONTENTMENT

*A Handbook for Meditation
and Spiritual Freedom*

JEFF CARREIRA

EMERGENCE EDUCATION
Philadelphia, Pennsylvannia

ISBN: 978-0-9995658-6-5

Emergence Education
P.O. Box 63767
Philadelphia, PA 19147
EmergenceEducation.com

Cover and interior design by Sophie Peirce.

Printed in the United States of America.

"And I, I myself, am the center that exists only because the geometry of the abyss demands it; I am the nothing around which all this spins, I exist so that it can spin, I am a center that exists only because every circle has one."

— FERNANDO PESSOA

Contents

Forward. 1

1: Becoming Unhookable 5

2: Opening To All Of Life. 15

3: Letting Go Of Mental Chatter 25

4: Giving Up Control Of The Journey 35

5: It's Already Here Just Beyond What
Your Mind Can See 47

6: There's No Need To Watch Yourself Meditate . . .57

7: You Are The Awareness That Sees 69

8: Are You Ready For A Better Life? 81

About the Author 91

Forward

JEFF CARREIRA IS ONE of the finest voices I know for making spiritual awakening not only accessible but touchable and close, without sacrificing its sacredness or a sense of due reverence. He is an emissary to the ordinary and extraordinary, the grounded and the transcendent facets of existence. He brings a quality of almost childlike wonder to his observations about reality, our own true nature, awakening and enlightenment, while embodying the authority and wisdom bestowed by decades of practice and inquiry. I love the simplicity and directness of his delivery as he parses often confounding perspectives or paradoxes.

Reading Jeff's writing — like hearing him speak — is an experience of making the previously opaque transparent (like the simple opening of a window), of having both a friend and a seasoned guide on the brave and exciting journey of awakening to who we always were, and a precious reminder of the miracle and mystery of being alive. Jeff is not afraid to challenge us and the illusions and habits that are innate to human nature and the mind, and yet his ever-present humility and compassion create an inviting sense of being in the epicenter of the adventure by his side rather than receiving pronouncements from the top down. Open your eyes and your mind with Jeff's generous and expansive treatment of spiritual life, and the paradoxes of the path will be something to discover and celebrate with wonder, instead of to struggle with or fear.

— *Robyn Landis,*
Certified trainer, coach, author and speaker.

Becoming Unhookable

IN THIS BOOK, YOU'LL find a comprehensive introduction to a form of meditation that I call The Practice of No Problem. The goal of this meditation is to release our awareness from its compulsive habits of fear, worry and self-concern, and, if we choose, to follow it to profound heights of spiritual freedom and illumination.

The Practice of No Problem can be taught to anyone in about ten seconds. The instructions are simply to sit and not make a problem out of anything that happens. Period. That's it. That's all the instruction you need.

It is literally as simple as that. Once the meditation begins, you simply don't make a problem out of any- thing that happens. And then, just to make absolutely certain you don't end up with a problem, once the meditation is over, you conclude that nothing went wrong and forget about whatever happened during your practice. That's it.

Go ahead and try it for five seconds or so. You'll find that it's so easy to have no problem for a few seconds, but to have no problem for an hour can seem almost impossible. What's the difference? What happens over the course of an hour that makes us increasingly certain that something is wrong?

What happens is that you get hooked on nagging thoughts that keep tempting you to think you've got a problem, and eventually you become convinced that something is wrong. The only thing that makes this meditation difficult is that we think meditation should feel a certain way, and unless we feel that way, we assume something is wrong. As long as you believe that your experience in meditation should be one way and not another, you'll keep getting caught in beliefs about something being wrong.

Meditation done in the form presented in this book can help diminish our anxiety and existential confusion and, at the same time, increase our focus, sense of peace and well-being. The reason this meditation can have such a positive effect on us is because so many of our troubles are caused by the same cultural habit of assuming that something is wrong.

We've been trained to believe that something is either already wrong or will go wrong soon, and so, we've learned to protect ourselves by staying on guard most of the time. The result is that we have adopted an inner posture toward life that is a little pulled back, relentlessly defensive, and always busy scrutinizing things to make sure they're safe. We end up feeling suffocated in a straightjacket made up of our fears and concerns, and we want to be free.

In this book, you'll learn how to break the habit of assuming something is wrong so you can live a more open, easy, free and spontaneous life. Even more importantly, you'll discover that life works out much better that way.

Your journey to inner freedom won't be easy because, as soon as you start to let go of the assumption that something is wrong, a part of you will start to argue that it is. And the arguments will sound very convincing. As that voice keeps arguing with you, you will be more and more tempted to concede and give up, but don't. The miracle will come if you persevere. My first piece of advice to you is: Don't quit before the miracle happens.

Like almost everyone else who starts to meditate, I used to think that meditation would quiet my mind and make my nagging thoughts go away. After medi- tating for about twelve years, anywhere from one to eight hours a day with periodic long retreats, I finally realized that my mind wasn't changing. It was just as neurotic as it ever was. And it dawned on me that maybe it was never going to change. I started to get depressed thinking that all that practice had been a waste of time. But then a miracle happened - I realized that even if my mind never stops, I don't have to listen to it.

The first miracle of meditation is the realization that your mental habits don't have to go away in order for you to be free of them. As soon as you learn to stop paying attention to your mind, you will realize that you were never anxious, worried or self-concerned. Your mind is all of those things from time to time, and if you keep listening to it, you'll think that's you, but the truth is you are not your mind.

The bottom line is that we're incredibly reactive to our minds and in meditation we get to see how our minds keep hooking us over and over again. They try to hook us one way then another, always wanting us to worry about something. If we don't take the bait, they just try another approach until we do.

The normal cycle of meditation goes something like this: You start out determined not to make a problem out of anything. Then you get caught on something. Then you free yourself, then you get caught again. And so on, and so on. The goal is to keep going until you are free of all mental reactivity - not because mental activity has stopped, but because you can't get hooked anymore.

In meditation, you learn to be unhookable. That means that no matter what your mind is doing, you are open, easy and free. What you will discover though, as soon as you start the practice, is that the temptation to get hooked is hard to resist. You're going to get hooked by your mind over and over and over again, but that doesn't matter because meditation is not about being unhooked, it's about being unhookable, and those are two different things. When you no longer get hooked by getting hooked, you'll be unhookable.

The most important thing you need to understand about meditation is that it's all about becoming unhookable and that means being OK even when you get hooked. That's the secret.

Don't worry if this doesn't totally make sense to you yet, or if you can't believe it's even possible. It will be clear by the end of this short book.

JEFF CARREIRA

The miracle will come if you persevere. My first piece of advice to you is: Don't quit before the miracle happens.

JEFF CARREIRA

CHAPTER TWO

Opening To All Of Life

IN THE LAST CHAPTER, we began our exploration of The Practice of No Problem meditation.
The first instruction for that practice is not to make
a problem out of anything you experience from the
time your meditation begins until it ends. The second instruction is that once the meditation ends,
you conclude that nothing when wrong and forget
about what happened. I added the second instruction because even if you don't make a problem out
of anything that happens during meditation, you
can still go back and replay your experience later
and make a problem out of it then.

This sounds so easy that you might be wonder-
ing if it's some kind of trick, but it's not. It actually
is as easy as it sounds. In fact, it's actually even easier
than it sounds. The challenge you face is not that
it's harder than it sounds. The challenge is that most
of us find it difficult to allow this meditation to be
as easy as it is.

The inner peace and clarity that you seek can be yours, and it doesn't have to take any time at all. The truth is that it may not happen today. It may not happen next week. It might not even happen over the next ten years. But whenever it happens, it will happen in an instant. You don't move gradually into inner clarity and deep peace. It comes whole and complete. Inner clarity and deep peace is not something that develops and grows, it's something we choose. And that choice doesn't have to wait because, as we've already said, nothing that bothers you needs to go away before you can be free; you just have to learn how to not be bothered by being bothered.

What takes time is getting to the point where you want to make that choice. What we typically call the spiritual path is whatever time and effort it takes for us to get to the point where we finally decide to let go and be free. The choice to be free is simply a choice to be OK with the way things are, no matter how they are, and you can always make that choice if you want to. Meditation is a practice of conscious contentment, which means consciously choosing to be content with things exactly the way they already are.

If you aren't ready to be at peace with the way things are, you will stay busy trying to make things the way you think they need to be so you can feel peaceful. As long as this is the case, you'll be a victim of circumstance, because you'll be insisting that your contentment is dependent on the circumstances around you.

The most supremely direct path to peace is to allow this moment, the one you are living right now as you read these words, to be the one when you finally decide to be content with the way things are, forever. Your mind will likely give you a multitude of reasons why this won't work, but if it does, you simply choose to be content with that too.

Let me share a dramatic story that illustrates the power of this meditation.

Six years ago I got a call from the hospital. They said that my wife had been in a terrible car accident and I needed to come to the hospital right away. I was in no shape to drive, so a friend drove me to the hospital. On the way, my mind kept running through all of the worst case scenarios in gruesome detail. My body was trembling with fear. Then, at one point, I asked myself: If one of these scenarios turns out to be true will that make life bad? And, in that moment, I knew that life would still be good. My life might be bad, but life itself would still be good. Existence itself would still be worth it, and from that moment on, I felt that I was ready for whatever I would find. The panic and trembling in my body didn't stop, and my mind continued displaying images of worst case scenarios, but I was ready.

A strong practice of meditation should leave you ready to face whatever life brings you. And when you're ready for anything, you're at peace, because you know that whatever happens, you're going to deal with it as best you can. From this state of readiness, even your wife's car accident isn't a problem, it's just a situation to deal with. You might desperately want it to be otherwise, but it is the way it is. It's a circumstance, and if you are ready, then you'll just deal with it.

When I got to the hospital, I found out that her story was much more remarkable than mine. After a head-on collision with a semi-trailer truck, she was pinned in her car for forty-five minutes listening to grinding metal, as rescue workers cut her out of the wreckage. She knew that if she panicked she was going to hurt herself, and she could hear how hard the rescue workers were struggling to save her. She felt that for her own well-being, and to help the rescuers be successful, she had to stay calm. So she meditated, following her breath until they were done. She had sustained terrible injuries, but over time, her positive attitude, hard work and inner peace led to a remarkable recovery.

I want to be clear, meditation isn't only about being ready when things are bad. It's about being ready all the time. Meditation is about being open to all of life, the good and the bad. The question you need to ask yourself is: Am I willing to be totally available for whatever life brings? Ordinarily, we're available for the good parts of life but not for the bad parts. Unfortunately, it doesn't really work that way. You can only open to all of life or none of it. Opening to life is like widening the lens of a camera, it opens in all directions at once. As you open to more of what's positive, you inevitably become sensitive to more of what is negative. This may sound scary, but you'll find that being open is always better than being closed. Being available for the good and the bad is better than shrinking from life as a whole.

The open space and contentment that you discover in meditation becomes the foundation upon which you can open to all of life. When you do, you're ready to meet even your worst moments fully. And when things are going great, you're ready to allow them to be as good as they are.

*Opening to life is like widening
the lens of a camera, it opens
in all directions at once. As you
open to more of what's positive,
you inevitably become sensitive
to more of what is negative. This
may sound scary, but you'll find
that being open is always better
than being closed. Being available
for the good and the bad is better
than shrinking from life as a
whole.*

CHAPTER THREE:

Letting Go Of Mental Chatter

THE MOST COMMON CHALLENGE we face in meditation are the problems we tend to have with thought; namely, that we keep getting lost in thought. We have all these chattering voices in our heads talking to us all the time. They chatter on and on about everything, and we keep getting stuck in whatever they're saying.

Of all the voices we might hear in our heads, the trickiest one to deal with during meditation is the one that pretends to be our own personal inner meditation coach. It tells us what we're doing right and what we're doing wrong. It encourages us to do more of this and to stop doing that. It appears to be trying to help us learn how to meditate and do it right.

We'll call this the coaching-voice and eventually the coaching-voice will tell you not to listen to all the other mental chatter. It will tell you that you need to get rid of the other chattering voices before you can really meditate, but it will keep right on chattering away.

So here's the secret: The coaching-voice is just another chattering voice in disguise.

We know the chattering voices are annoying, but we tend to think about the coaching-voice differently. We think it is us talking to ourselves. It doesn't feel like just another chattering voice, but it is. When we mistakenly believe that the coaching-voice is us talking to ourselves, we're identifying with it and we give our power away to it. Suddenly, it's not just a voice in our head that weccan ignore. Now it's us sharing our own insights with ourselves. We can't ignore it, because it's us.

In order to truly meditate, we have to realize that none of the voices in our heads are us. None of them are really us talking to ourselves. They are thoughts created by the mind that we have been trained to identify with, and so we assume they're us talking to ourselves.

The coaching voice is no different than any other mental chatter and, just like all the rest, it's coming from a mind that's been trained to assume that something's wrong. So, if we think that voice is us, sooner or later we'll start believing that we have a problem. But if we don't listen, if we just let it go, then it can't bother us.

At this point, it will be valuable to consider what exactly it means to have no problem with thought. Often we think, mainly because our coaching-voice tells us so, that to have no problem all the inner voices would have to go away. But not having a problem simply means not caring whether the voices are there and not caring whether we get caught in them or not. If you don't care if the voices are there, and you don't care if you get caught in them, then you can't possibly have a problem with them. Everything is fine just the way it is, no matter how it is.

Ultimately, this meditation practice means being completely passive and not doing anything at all. If you learn to unconditionally stop doing anything about anything, eventually you'll realize that you never were doing anything. Whatever it is that you think you're doing in the privacy of you mind is just something that's happening. The only way to see this completely is to learn how to unconditional stop doing anything at all. When you do, you will discover that absolutely nothing changes once you've stopped doing anything. All the mental chatter keeps on going; even the getting caught in thought keeps on going. You've stopped and yet everything continues. That could only mean that you were never doing any of it in the first place.

Letting go of mental chatter in meditation does not mean making it stop. It means recognizing that every voice in your head is just mental chatter - that none of it is you talking to yourself - and then just not listening anymore.

Let this be as simple as it sounds. When you're meditating, just don't make a problem out of anything. You'll start hearing the voices of mental chatter. You'll start to hear the instruction of the coaching-voice. One voice tells you about something that's wrong, another voice tells you not to listen to that voice, still another voice tells you that all the other voices don't know what they're talking about. You'll hear voices telling you you're bored, others telling you this won't work, maybe even some telling you this is wonderful and you're almost free. The symphony of voices will go on and on and on, and you just let it all happen, watching them like small birds chirping and flitting around.

If you do this completely enough something wonderful will start to happen: You'll lose interest in what any of the voices are saying. You've already decided not to pay attention to them, so why bother even listening to find out what you already know you're going to ignore. If you honestly know that you're not going to react to anything that they say, then there's no reason to listen at all. On the other hand, if you leave even a little room for the possibility that one voice might say something worth paying attention to, then you're going to feel compelled to listen to each and every one of them to be sure you can ignore it.

You can do this practice by checking each and every voice first to see what it says and then letting it go and ignoring what it says, but that gets to be exhausting and you'll probably end up giving up over time and missing the miracle. The miracle only happens when you know, in your heart of hearts, that during meditation you're not going to listen to any of the voices, without exception. That's when you give yourself permission to ignore all of them completely. That's when you stop even checking first to see what they say. And that's how you really let go of mental chatter - by discovering that none of the voices in your head are you talking to yourself.

JEFF CARREIRA

Letting go of mental chatter in meditation does not mean making it stop. It means recognizing that every voice in your head is just mental chatter - that none of it is you talking to yourself - and then just not listening anymore.

CHAPTER FOUR:

Giving Up Control
Of The Journey

IN THE FIRST THREE chapters of this book, my goal was to support you in discovering how to break the habit of assuming that something is wrong using the Practice of No Problem meditation. You learned how to break the habits of mental reactivity so that you could discover for yourself that nothing that happens in your mind is anything more than just-stuff happening. This profound freedom from reactivity liberates you from a huge source of insecurity and anxiety. You can take what you have learned already and use it to live a much happier and more spontaneously free life right now.

If, on the other hand, you feel compelled to go deeper with the practice, you will discover that freedom from mental reactivity, as wonderful as it is, is only the beginning of a much larger journey. If you follow this practice all the way to the end, you'll discover a place that is inherently free and at ease and always has been. In that place, you never had a problem because no problems ever exist.

Beyond the attainment of inner contentment, you will find yourself walking a path of ongoing spiritual illumination. As your practice deepens, you begin to experience cascades of insight into the secret mysteries of your true nature and the essential workings of life.

For the remainder of this book, we will expand our exploration beyond the limits of inner contentment to explore the practice of meditation as a journey of spiritual growth and awakening.

If you embrace The Practice of No Problem in earnest in the ways we have already described, sooner or later, you will discover that everything you think, and everything you think you're doing, is just some other thing that's happening. You will realize that it is all just happening and that you were never doing any of it. The practice of meditation means giving up control and discovering, when you do, that we were never in control in the first place.

Once in meditation, it occurred to me that I didn't have to try to control my breathing, so I just stopped trying to breathe. What I discovered was that my body goes right on breathing even when I stop trying to breathe. My body, and yours, are perfectly capable of breathing all on their own without any help from us. This little experience of letting go of the process of breathing serves as a great metaphor for the giving up of control that meditation is.

In meditation, the thing we find ourselves trying to control over and over again is our experience. We want to have a pleasant experience rather than an unpleasant one. We want to feel peace and calm, rather than frustration or boredom. We want to have a spiritual experience or energetic opening, or at least go to a deeper place in consciousness.

Our meditation tends to be full of attempts to make something happen. Some of those attempts are conscious and deliberate, others are unconscious habits, but in the end they are all about trying to guide our own awakening process. Underneath all of our conscious and unconscious efforts to manipulate our experience is an assumption that our awakening won't happen unless we make it happen. This is a very subtle form of having a problem. We assume that growth will not happen unless we intervene.

Spiritually speaking, The Practice of No Problem is based in the recognition that our awakening is already happening, and that it will happen best if we stop trying to control it. Life grows all by itself. Seeds become trees, babies become adults. Everywhere you look, growth happens all by itself, and what I'm telling you now is that spiritual growth is no exception.

Our spiritual awakening and growth will inevitably continue as long as we don't act in ways that stop it. In fact, in the long run, we can't avoid it, because no matter what happens, life always finds a new way to continue onward. When you learn how to give up control, you'll find that there are mysterious forces in the universe working for your awakening. We thwart our own awakening by trying to control and guide it ourselves.

Imagine having a smart car that has been designed to drive itself. It already knows where to go and how to get there. It's guided by a G.P.S. system and it's completely self-controlled, but you won't let go of the wheel. You keep driving off the road. Then one day you take your hands off the wheel, certain that you will crash, but you don't. Instead you find that the wheel turns all by itself.

The car drives itself beautifully and you don't need to do anything except keep your hands off the wheel. This is a perfect metaphor for spiritual surrender. It means you give up trying to control your awakening process and allow yourself to be guided by forces that you cannot see.

We live in a buoyant spiritual atmosphere, lifted and supported in ways we can't understand. If you're in water, the water carries you to the surface effortlessly. If we keep struggling to get to the surface, we might exhaust ourselves and end up drinking in so much water that we drown; but if we lay calmly on our backs and continue to breathe, the water will hold us up.

In meditation we find that, if we let go, we start to feel ourselves being moved. We don't all move at the same speed. Some of us rise upward more quickly, some more slowly, but every one of us floats.

Spiritually we're always being taken further. The thing that gets in the way is that we think we can make it go faster, or smoother, or better, by taking control of the process. The biggest obstacle to spiritual growth is that we think we can do it better ourselves and we miss the fact that it's all already happening perfectly in ways we just don't understand.

It's all already happening. We're already here. We're already alive. We're already conscious and awake. This is it! In the midst of all this perfection, our mind sometimes makes noise that is unpleasant. Yes, it would be more pleasant if your mind was quiet, and if you meditate enough you'll have those moments. And that's great. I prefer meditation when my mind is quiet too.

I also know it doesn't happen that often. I meditate everyday and, during most of them, my mind is busy chattering away. It makes sense if you think about it. If we spend most of our time with a busy mind getting things done, why would we imagine that it would come to a dead stop during the few minutes that we decided to meditate? Minds are not that well behaved. If you go on a retreat and you meditate all day for a few days, your mind will start to get quiet. Eventually, it will stop generating any thoughts at all, and that's wonderful. But does it really matter? If you're not bothered by your thoughts, then it doesn't really matter whether they're there or not.

Most of the world will pressure you to feel like there's something wrong all the time; they will tell you that you need to do more, be better, and work harder to get what you want. And in terms of many of the things that we want, that is the way the world works. But, at the existential level that we're exploring here, it doesn't work that way. Because at these depths, everything is already fine no matter how it seems. You're here. You're alive. You're conscious. And you're in the middle of a journey of awakening that is beyond what your mind can comprehend.

When you learn how to give up control, you'll find that there are mysterious forces in the universe working for your awakening.

CHAPTER FIVE

It's Already Here Just Beyond What Your Mind Can See

THE ONLY THING THAT keeps you from having the spiritual openings and realizations that you want is your belief that you're not already having them. Without realizing it, most of us are busy actively insisting that this moment of meditation is not the experience of peace, calm and wholeness that we're looking for. We disqualify this moment, and then we move on in search of the right one. What we don't realize is that this insatiable search is exactly what keeps us from feeling peaceful and whole.

The reason we keep disqualifying the present moment is because we have some idea about what we think we're looking for, and we measure every moment against whatever we think. Inevitably, the actual moment doesn't match up to whatever fantasy we have about it and so we keep looking.

If we want to discover the true depths that meditation offers, we have to give up everything we think we know about how it works and where it leads. Even if we're right, and our ideas match reality as we know it, we still have to give them up, because in the end, reality is bigger than any of our ideas about it. What you are seeking is not just something you can know with your mind. It's much more than that. Your mind is never going to be able to hold it, but you can.

This all gets much easier once you know, beyond any doubt, that you are not your mind. You never were your mind. You were always much more than your mind. You were trained to identify with your mind and to see yourself as the thinker of your thoughts. Because we think that we are our minds, we assume that the freedom we seek must exist inside our minds. We can't imagine that anything the mind can't recognize could possibly be it.

How do we let go of all of our ideas about how meditation works and where it leads? You do it by not worrying about how you feel or what you think. The peace and calm that you seek is much bigger than a peaceful and calm mind. The miracle of meditation is that you can be peaceful and calm, no matter what your mind feels or thinks.

The challenge is that you have to be open to the existence of a miracle that you may not be able to recognize. It doesn't feel like what you thought it would, so you don't see it at all. If you find a way to be open to a mystery that is beyond what your mind can know, you'll find yourself being calm and peaceful no matter what your mind is doing. You won't be able to say when you feel this way, but it is true just the same. This is true freedom.

As long as you hold on to any ideas about how meditation works and where it leads, you will have a very difficult time becoming unhookable, because as soon as you start to experience something that feels like what you were expecting, you'll think: "Yes! This is it." Then, you'll want to figure out what it is and how you got there and how you can keep it. As soon as you start thinking this way, it will be gone and you'll realize you've lost it, and then you'll try to get it back.

If you're lucky, at some point, you'll get so tired of this that you'll give up trying and then: Boom! It will be right here waiting for you. As long as you are invested in knowing what it is and how to get it, you'll end up stuck in unending loops trying to figure it out. These cycles of glimpsing the miracle and losing it again will continue until you stop caring about what it is and how to get it. Everything you want is already here anyway as soon as you stop trying to know it or understand it.

We've been trained to search for answers with our minds. When we have a problem to solve or a question to answer, we focus on our thoughts until the answer appears. We tend to bring this habit of fixating our attention on the mind to our spiritual practice as well, but the spiritual answers we seek are not located in our mind.

If you stop looking toward your mind to find it, you'll see it everywhere all around you. As long as you don't try to know it or understand it, you'll see that you're swimming in it all the time. It's like something you can only see out of the corner of your eye. You see it out just beyond the edges of your vision, but as soon as you turn to look at it straight on, it's gone. As long as you try to see it clearly, it remains out of view. But if you're willing to not see it clearly, then you can finally relax, knowing that it's always there at the edges.

The biggest obstacle to what we seek is that we want to know it, to see it, to have it. We don't want to be awake and free. What we really want is to know that we're awake and free. Being something, and knowing that you are it, are two different things. Being something has to do with what you are, while knowing something has to do with what your mind sees and understands about what you are. They are not the same thing.

You are already awake and free. Your mind never will be. As long as you believe that you cannot be awake and free unless your mind is, then the struggle will never end. As soon as you are ready to be awake and free right now, no matter what your mind thinks and feels, you'll immediately discover that you are already.

We're talking about letting go of any motivation in us that wants to have an awakening as if it were something that we could possess, because awakening is not something we can possess - it's only something we can be.

As you start to understand that the true goal of meditation is not something you are ever going to be able to have and hold onto, there may be a part of you that starts to wonder if the practice is worth all the effort. If the big realization ends up being that it's all already here right now, just the way things are, then why bother doing any practice? The pain, suffering and monotony I'm experiencing in life is exactly what I want to escape from, and now you're telling me that there is no better life at the other end of the practice.

That is not exactly what I am saying though.

What I'm really saying is that you'll see that your life, exactly the way it is, is already amazing as you start truly living it, rather than trying to escape it.

If you stop looking toward your mind to find it, you'll see it everywhere all around you. As long as you don't try to know it or understand it, you'll see that you're swimming in it all the time.

CHAPTER SIX

There's No Need To Watch Yourself Meditate

WHEN YOU MEDITATE, YOU start at a certain time and then you end at a later time. Once the meditation starts, you simply don't make a problem out of anything that happens until it's over. And when it's over, you conclude that nothing went wrong and move on and forget about it. With those instructions, there is literally no way to do it wrong.

Since these instructions ask you not to make a problem, we should take a minute to get clear about what exactly it means to make a problem in the first place. If you think about it, the only way that you make a problem out of something is by insisting that it's a problem. You make problems by calling something a problem. Having a problem is a distinctly human activity. In the non-human natural world, there are no problems. There are just things happening. There are situations, events and circumstances, and none of it is a problem. It just is.

It isn't all pleasant to look at; little animals get eaten by big animals and others get diseases and die. Of course, some of it is beautiful, like flowers blooming or the sun flashing red out beyond the horizon. The idea that any of it is a problem is just that, an idea.

When we say something is a problem, what we really mean is that it's not the way it should be. And the only way we can conclude that something is wrong is by knowing how it should be. To have a problem, you must first have an idea of the way things should be that you can compare to the way they are. We insist there is a problem when the way things are is not the way we think they should be.

We create problems by comparing the way things are to the way we think they should be. We are constantly, consciously and unconsciously, comparing everything to what we think it should be. This relentless evaluation of reality is what causes so much anxiety, and our level of anxiety increases in direct proportion with the gap between the way things are and the way we think they should be.

If you want to rid yourself of unnecessary anxiety, there's two things you can do: You can try to make sure that everything is always the way you think it should be, or you can let go of any ideas you have that things should be other than the way they are.

We have been conditioned to operate in the first way, and so we constantly try to make everything be the way we think it should be. Anyone reading this book has undoubtedly already realized living this way is the cause of anxiety, not the solution for it.

If we choose to live the second way, we simply stop thinking about the way things should be and, instead, just respond to the way they are. That doesn't mean everything's going to magically be the way we want it to be. Everything will go on being exactly the way it is. Some things will be painful and we're going to want to act to alleviate the pain. Some things will be exactly how we think they should be and we won't need to do anything with them at all. I am not saying that having no problem means magically liking everything the way it is. There is nothing wrong with trying to make things the way we want them to be as long as we learn how to not make a problem out of the way they are.

This is subtle so go slow; I'm not saying that we have to learn how to be content with pain, or suffering, or injustice. We just have to learn how to not have a problem with the fact that we sometimes experience pain, suffering and injustice even though we don't ever want to. We're not going to make a problem out of any of that anymore because we know that is just the way it is and we have given up the idea that it should be some other way. We have learned to step back and allow everything to be as it is, even the things we don't like and want to be different.

When you're sitting in meditation, you're just experiencing whatever is there and you're not concluding that any of it is wrong, even when your mind keeps on saying things are wrong. You're going to allow your mind's habitual judgments to happen without concluding that those are wrong either. You'll be experiencing whatever you're experiencing, and your mind will be making whatever judgements it makes, and you'll be totally content with the whole thing. Why? Because that is just the way it is and there's no other way that it should be.

The meditation asks you to not make a problem out of anything, and this is literally what you're doing.

We make problems by taking things that just are and calling them problems. We make problems by calling things problems. We stop making problems when we stop calling things problems. That doesn't mean we like everything we see. It just means we accept it as it is. And we have to do this even if our mind doesn't. In meditation, you'll see your mind calling things problems even though you've decided that you're not going to do that. Your mind will say that things are not the way they should be, and there's no reason to stop your mind from doing that. You just have to learn to be OK with the fact that it does.

In your meditation, you sit and inevitably something will arise that your mind will say is wrong. Then, you'll remind yourself not to make a problem out of it, and you'll relax and let go, until something else arises that your mind says is wrong. Your meditation will continue in these cycles until the end. As you put more time into practice, you will go longer and longer times between problems.

This is not yet the true practice.

At some point, you'll realize that even seeing your mind having a problem and then remembering to let it go is not a problem. It doesn't matter if you go through these cycles. There is no reason for you to worry about any of that. Just let it happen.

This is when the meditation gets brutally simple, because now you're not going to make a problem out of literally anything. You're just going to live through the experience of whatever happens. You'll sit in meditation for 10, 15, or 30 minutes, and when the meditation ends, no matter what's happened, you're just going to get up and forget about it.

At this point something will dawn on you: Since nothing that could possibly happen will ever be a problem, there's no reason to even pay attention to what happens.

Why bother paying attention? There's no reason to watch yourself having the experience you're having. So you can stop paying attention to whatever's happening. We live our lives constantly watching ourselves live them at the same time. The watcher is constantly commenting on everything that happens, but there's no reason to watch what's happening if nothing that happens could possibly be wrong. You're free from the need to monitor your own experience, and a whole new level of practice opens up.

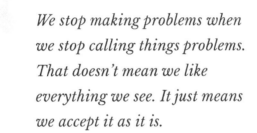

We stop making problems when we stop calling things problems. That doesn't mean we like everything we see. It just means we accept it as it is.

CHAPTER SEVEN

You Are The Awareness That Sees

THE TYPE OF MEDITATION we're exploring in this book asks us not to make a problem out of anything that happens. That means that no matter what you experience in your practice, you just leave it exactly the way it is, including - and pay special attention to this - any of the ways that you see yourself trying to change things and solve problems.

If we are really letting absolutely everything be exactly the way it is, we will eventually start seeing through the illusions that our minds create. What we discover is that a great deal of what we experience as real is not. We already know this. We know that we sometimes hear someone say something, and realize later they said something else. We either misheard them or misinterpreted them. Our minds are constantly interpreting reality for us. The ultimate promise of meditation is that we will see beyond all of the mind's interpretations of reality until we finally see what is actually real. The key to achieving this profound level of perceptual clarity is learning to leave everything alone, including everything we think we're doing.

If you are truly going to leave everything exactly the way it already is, then what is the difference between meditating and anything else? At this depth of practice, the distinction between meditating and not meditating breaks down. You might reasonably ask, "If I'm not going to do anything about anything, then what is the use of meditating?"

"What about daydreaming?" You could continue, "If I'm just sitting here daydreaming about my next vacation, is that meditating?" Actually yes it is, but only if you don't do anything with it. If you find yourself daydreaming in meditation, you don't do anything about it. You allow the daydreaming to continue. Of course, once you notice it happening, you might find yourself doing something to end the daydream so you can refocus on your practice. If you see yourself doing this, then you just let that happen too. Neither is better or worse than the other. They are both just things that happen. In meditation, we have no preference for having any experience over any other.

Leaving everything alone in this way gets very tricky because some parts of what we experience we think are us doing things. When we see ourselves daydreaming, or ending a daydream, or refocusing our practice, or reminding ourselves of the instructions, or trying to solve a problem, or any other of an infinite number of things we might discover ourselves doing, we naturally conclude that we have stopped meditating. We are supposed to be letting everything be as it is, and so, when we see ourselves getting involved with something, we feel like we have stopped meditating and need to restart the practice.

But what you need to realize is that seeing yourself doing something is just another experience that is happening. If we have a random thought, it's pretty easy to just let it be. But, if we see ourselves getting involved with something, we find it hard not to assume that we have stopped following the instruction. After all, didn't we just do something?

If you think deeply about it, you will see that all of the things that appear to be you doing something are themselves just more experiences to not get involved with. We can let those be, just as easily as we can our random thoughts. Understanding this is the key to experiencing profound meditation. It's hard to explain because it is so subtle, but I'll try anyway.

We are all trained to see a split in reality. We habitually separate our experience into two parts. One part is just stuff that happens that doesn't have anything to do with us. We will call this the just-stuff category. The other part includes everything that we perceive to be me doing stuff. We'll call this the me-stuff category. So we split our experience into just-stuff and me-stuff. The secret to profound meditation is recognizing that the me-stuff is also just-stuff.

As far as meditation goes, nothing that happens in your head is you doing stuff. It is all just stuff happening.

Meditation is a profound learning opportunity, and everything that happens is part of the learning process. Even daydreaming is something you learn from. I'm not talking about learning from the content of the daydream; what the daydream is about is irrelevant. What you're learning is about how your mind works. That's what you're always learning about in meditation. You're seeing how your mind continually moves in and out of thoughts, memories, daydreams and feeling sensations, over and over again. You're not trying to control your mind. You're not trying to make it behave. You're just observing it, so you can see exactly how it works when you're not doing anything with it.

When you do this, you discover something amazing. Your mind works exactly the same way whether you're trying to control it or not. If you give up controlling your mind and just let everything be exactly as it is, you'll discover that nothing changes. That's because you were never in control of your mind in the first place. When you see this, you will have seen through one of the most captivating illusions that the mind creates - the illusion that you are in control of your mental processes.

When we meditate, we often prefer it when we experience a calm, peaceful, empty mind. In these pleasant experiences of meditation, very few thoughts arise. We feel that we're being carried along on a gentle current, floating lazily down a river. These are indeed the most pleasant meditations, but they are not the most valuable ones.

The meditations that most of us find difficult - the ones where we keep seeing ourselves getting lost in thought over and over again, then seeing ourselves reminding ourselves that we are meditating and refocusing, and then remembering that there's no need to do that because the practice is to let everything be exactly the way it is, etc. - these are the unpleasant, monkey mind meditations that most of us want to avoid, but these challenging meditations are actually the most valuable ones.

If we can get to the point where we can be perfectly content with all that mental chatter and self-conscious engagement without identifying with any of it, then we're not just breaking the habit of mental reactivity, we're also breaking the habit of separating our mind into just-stuff and me-stuff. Eventually, it will be obvious to us that there is no me-stuff, there is only just-stuff. Everything that happens in your mind is just-stuff happening. None of it is you. There is nothing in there that we can see that is us. We are the perceiver, and we can never see ourselves. We are never what we see, we are always the awareness that sees.

We are the perceiver, and we can never see ourselves. We are never what we see, we are always the awareness that sees.

CHAPTER EIGHT

Are You Ready For A Better Life?

ANOTHER WAY TO UNDERSTAND meditation is to understand that it's just about giving up control and surrendering to whatever is. Whatever happens is going to happen and you're not going to do anything about it. Some part of you might start to freak out as if it is walking into an enemy camp unarmed. Of course, the miracle is that you find out that there is no enemy - at least not in your head.

What makes it so difficult to let go in meditation is the fact that, ultimately, we can't really let go in meditation more than we're willing to let go in life. You are the same person in meditation as you are in life. If you're attached to things in life and you don't want them to change, then you're not going to be able to give up control in meditation because you'll worry that, if you let go in meditation, you might start to let go in life too.

In the end, you can't limit meditation to just the time you sit. You can if you keep the practice more superficial. You can keep your practice superficial by limiting it to just getting better at recognizing that you are caught in a problem and getting yourself out of it. If you develop the habit of recognizing when you're caught in a problem and then getting out of it, that alone will have a dramatically positive effect on your life. And if you can keep it to that, you won't be risking too much upset in your life. But, if you really want to go deeply into the practice, so deeply that you start questioning who you are, well then, you can't really control where this adventure will take you.

If your meditation practice gets deep enough, you'll start seeing through the mind's illusory preferences and biases. You'll start seeing yourself and your life more accurately. If there are things that you don't want to change, you aren't going to want to see them more clearly. You'll be afraid that you won't like what you see and that you'll have to change them.

Of course, it's also good to remember that there isn't anything in your life that you necessarily have to change, but if you want to be free, then you have to be willing for anything in your life to change. If you want to follow this practice all the way to spiritual freedom, there can't be anything in your life that you are completely unwilling to question. If you think about your own life, certain things will likely appear to your mind's eye. These are usually the things that you tend to assume can't change. Usually these things include taking care of ourselves, taking care of our families, and earning a living.

When we think about the possibility of deep transformation and these things come to mind, we'll see how, when we start to let go of control, our minds insist that we should stop because we've got children, or we can't afford to give up our job, or something else can't change. Your mind is good at telling you how bad things will get if you change certain aspects of your life, but what it never considers is the possibility that things might get better. The whole reason we started meditating in the first place was because we wanted things to change. We knew things could be better and we wanted them to be.

Getting free of your mind doesn't make things worse. It makes them better. How could being free from your fearful habits be worse for your child, for yourself, for your family, and even for your work? In the end, being free of fear, worry, and self-concern would have to make things better for everyone.

We know that holding on is a problem. We know it's making us and people around us more miserable, but still we're afraid that, without it, things will fall apart and get worse. What we lack is faith - faith in life. The faith to know that if we relax and let go, our life will get better as a result.

You can work with meditation just as a practice that's limited to the times when you're sitting. You can get better at doing the practice and it will have positive effects on your life. But, if you're interested in more dramatic change, then in addition to doing the practice, you'll also want to be looking at your life to see what you're unwilling to change and then question- ing if it's possible that those things could get better. If you stop change because you're afraid things might get worse, you're also stopping them from the possibility of getting better.

In order to really experience the full transformative power of meditation, our practice has to include a sincere examination of our lives and what it would take for us to be willing to risk change. If you sit down in meditation and you're willing for anything to change, then you won't even be tempted to make a problem out or anything. What could be a problem if you aren't holding on to anything? If you're ready for anything to change, you can't help but be open and available for anything that comes your way.

Yet another way to think about meditation is to see it as the practice of being available for more. Being available to be moved in ways that we can't imagine yet. Ultimately, it means being available to be moved by the sacred and the divine. The divine wants to move us, but we're not available. We want to be free, we want to be available for more, but we have so much we need to do first. We're busy with our own agenda. We know there's a bigger life we're meant to live, and sometimes it feels so close we wonder why it isn't here already. Our full potential is always here waiting for us, as soon as we're available for it. As long as we're busy doing something else, we'll miss it.

Meditation is the practice of availability and being available is also the best way to live your life. When you're fully available, there's no difference between life and meditation. When you're available, your life will be guided by a consistent stream of insight and understanding. We don't get powerful insights about what is possible for us if we're not ready to act on them, but as soon as we're ready for them, the insights will come and a new life will unfold.

The reason we meditate is to be available to be carried forward into a better life. The purpose of meditation is to unstick ourselves from the mental habits of fearful control, so that we're free to be moved by the sacred and the divine. We can't stay in control and be guided at the same time. To be available for a better life, we have to let go.

To learn how to let go, you need to have a place where you can consciously practice releasing the habit of watching and controlling yourself. This is how you can discover what it means to be free.

Yet another way to think about meditation is to see it as the practice of being available for more. Being available to be moved in ways that we can't imagine yet. Ultimately, it means being available to be moved by the sacred and the divine.

About the Author

Jeff Carreira is a meditation teacher, mystical philosopher and author who teaches tirelessly to a growing number of people throughout the world. As a teacher, Jeff offers retreats and courses guiding individuals in a form of meditation called The Practice of No Problem. Through this simple and effective meditation technique, Jeff has led thousands of people in the journey beyond the confines of fear and self-concern into the expansive liberated awareness that is our true home.

Ultimately, Jeff is interested in defining a new way of being in the world that will move us from our current paradigm of separation and isolation into an emerging paradigm of unity and wholeness. He is exploring some of the most revolutionary ideas and systems of thought in the domains of spirituality, consciousness, and human development. He teaches people how to question their own experience so deeply that previously held assumptions about the nature of reality fall away to create space for dramatic shifts in understanding.

Jeff is passionate about philosophy because he is passionate about the power of ideas to shape how we perceive reality and how we live together. His enthusiasm for learning is infectious, and he enjoys addressing student groups and inspiring them to develop their own powers of inquiry. He has taught students at colleges and universities throughout the world.

Jeff is the author of numerous books including: *No Place But Home*, *The Miracle of Meditation*, *The Practice of No Problem*, *Embrace All That You Are*, *Philosophy Is Not a Luxury*, *Radical Inclusivity*, *The Soul of a New Self*, and *Paradigm Shifting*.

For more about Jeff visit: jeffcarreira.com or scan the QR code below.

Made in the USA
Las Vegas, NV
27 July 2024

92990860R00056